JOURNEY TO CUBEVILLE

JOURNEY TO CUBEVILLE

A DILBERT™ BOOK

BY **SCOTT ADAMS**

Andrews McMeel
Publishing

Kansas City

073494

For Pam "Ah likes to read" Okasaki

Other DILBERT books from Andrews McMeel Publishing

I'm Not Anti-Business, I'm Anti-Idiot
ISBN: 0-8362-5182-2

Seven Years of Highly Defective People
ISBN: 0-8362-3668-8 (ppb)
ISBN: 0-8362-5129-6 (hd)

Casual Day Has Gone Too Far
ISBN: 0-8362-2899-5

Fugitive from the Cubicle Police
ISBN: 0-8362-2119-2

Still Pumped from Using the Mouse
ISBN: 0-8362-1026-3

It's Obvious You Won't Survive by Your Wits Alone
ISBN: 0-8362-0415-8

Bring Me the Head of Willy the Mailboy!
ISBN: 0-8362-1779-9

Shave the Whales
ISBN: 0-8362-1740-3

Dogbert's Clues for the Clueless
ISBN: 0-8362-1737-3

Build a Better Life by Stealing Office Supplies
ISBN: 0-8362-1757-8

Always Postpone Meetings with Time-Wasting Morons
ISBN: 0-8362-1758-6

For ordering information, call 1-800-642-6480.

Introduction

Rather than fill this page with a frivolous book introduction that you would soon forget, I thought it would be better to answer all of your questions about the nature of the universe. It's more work for me, but you're worth it. Here are the questions I get most often:

Q: I'm a student studying to be an engineer. Is it my fate to sit in a cubicle?

A: No, it's unlikely that you'll be sitting. Recent studies show that if employees are piled like firewood, up to forty can be stored in one cubicle. It's not an ideal arrangement, but you'll get used to it. One thing they don't teach you in school is that you can get used to anything if someone forces you.

Q: Do praying mantises burp?

A: Yes, if they run with their mouths open. That causes huge air pockets to form in their thoraxes, not to mention their boraxes and their pickaxes. That air has to go someplace, otherwise the praying mantis becomes bigger and bigger until eventually it buys dark glasses and becomes Howard Stern. But that only happened once.

Q: Is the planet controlled by a secret society of highly intelligent people?

A: No, we don't like to think of ourselves as a "society." It's more of a cabal. By the way, what was your home address? We'd like to send you something.

Q: Where's the rest of the moon when it's not a full moon?

A: When they landed on the moon in 1969, the astronauts shoveled most of the moon's surface into special containers and took it home. They would have taken the whole thing, but they needed to keep some dirt there to hold the flag up. If you see something that looks like a full moon, that's either a false memory or someone playing a practical joke on you.

I hope that answers all of your questions. If I missed anything, I'll handle it in the next book. In the meantime, if you would like to join the cabal of highly intelligent people, it also goes by the name of Dogbert's New Ruling Class (DNRC). After Dogbert conquers the planet, he'll make everyone outside the DNRC our personal servants. If you're tired of getting up to fetch your own beverages, this is the solution for you. To become a member, all you need to do is put your name on the list to receive the totally free DNRC newsletter, which is published according to the rigorous "whenever I feel like it" schedule. That's about three or four times a year.

To subscribe, send e-mail to listserv@listserv.unitedmedia.com in the following format:

subject: newsletter
message: Subscribe Dilbert_News Firstname Lastname

Don't include any other information—your e-mail address will be picked up automatically.

If the automatic method doesn't work for you, you can also subscribe by writing to scottadams@aol.com or via snail mail:

Dilbert Mailing List
United Media
200 Madison Avenue
New York, NY 10016

These methods are much slower than the automatic method so please be patient.

S. Adams

Scott Adams

THE TEAM-BUILDING EXERCISE

UH-OH... I'M A MILE FROM SHORE AND TOO EXHAUSTED TO SWIM BACK.

MY ONLY HOPE IS THAT AN INTELLIGENT DOLPHIN WILL SEE MY PLIGHT AND RESCUE ME.

I'M IN LUCK!

TWO WORDS: TUNA... NET.

SOME DOLPHINS IN MY SITUATION WOULD HELP YOU GET TO SHORE SAFELY.

OTHERS MIGHT TRY TO DISTRACT YOU WHILE AN ACCOMPLICE PLAYED A CRUEL JOKE.

COME BACK HERE WITH MY TRUNKS!!!

LET'S ASK THE HUMMING FISH TO DO THE "JAWS" THEME SONG.

...THERE I WAS, NAKED AND EXHAUSTED, MILES FROM SHORE. DOLPHINS TAUNTED ME FOR HOURS.

SUDDENLY A DEEP SEA SPORT FISHING BOAT HAPPENED BY. I GRABBED THE LINE AND HELD ON FOR MY LIFE.

WOW! THAT'S LUCKY.

THAT'S WHAT I THOUGHT... UNTIL THE SECOND TIME THEY THREW ME BACK IN.

I MEANT LUCKY FOR THEM.

44

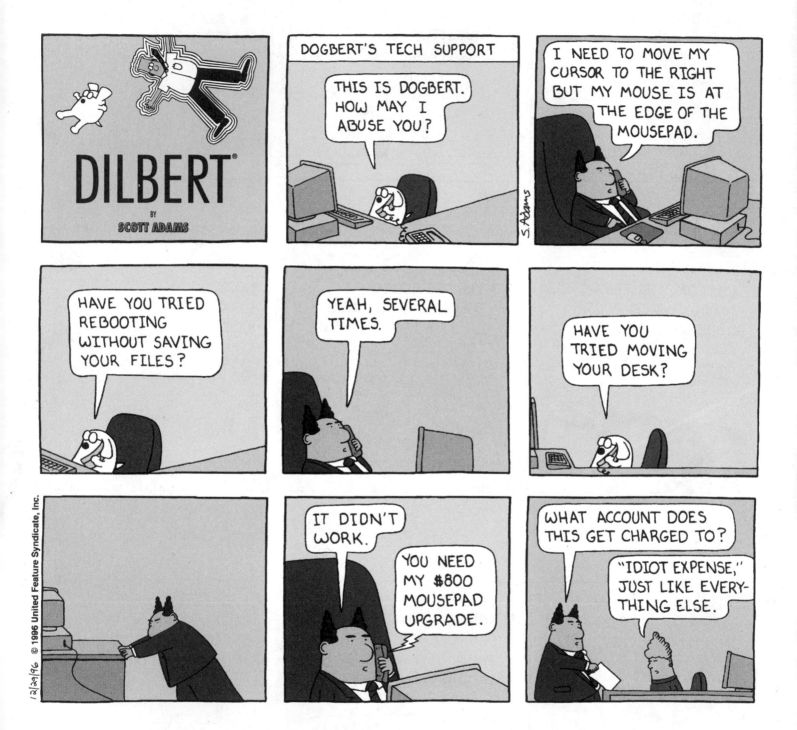

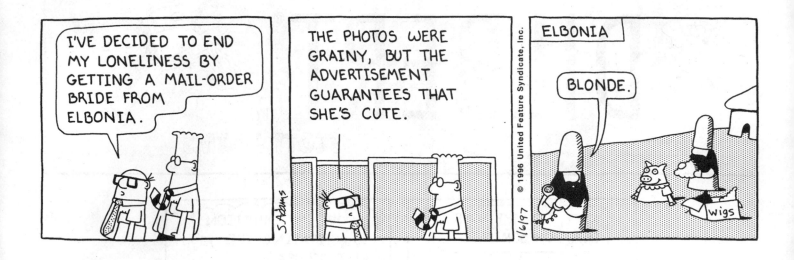

Editor's Note: On April Fool's Day, 1997, 46 syndicated cartoonists perpetrated a great hoax on newspaper comics readers by swapping strips for the day. One result was the above Dilbert strip. Scott Adams said of the swap-fest, "I think it was Nostradamus who predicted that when Pat Boone sings heavy metal and Bil Keane [Family Circus] draws Dilbert, it's a sign of the approaching apocalypse." (We say, "Duck!")

VISITING THE CUSTOMER

I BROUGHT DILBERT TO EXPLAIN WHAT MAKES OUR PRODUCT SPECIAL.

IT'S EXACTLY LIKE OUR COMPETITOR'S PRODUCT EXCEPT WE CHARGE MORE TO COVER THE COST OF OUR DECEPTIVE ADVERTISING.

WHILE YOU'RE UP, COULD YOU GET ME A CUP OF COFFEE?

VISITING THE CUSTOMER

NO ONE HAS EVER BEEN FIRED FOR BUYING OUR PRODUCT!

THAT'S TRUE.

THERE IS THE OCCASIONAL SAVAGE BEATING... AND MORE THAN OUR SHARE OF SUICIDES...

BUT THAT HAS "STATISTICAL CLUSTERING" WRITTEN ALL OVER IT.

SOMEDAY IT WILL BE POSSIBLE TO CLONE OUR BOSS.

BUT THE CLONE WOULD HAVE NO EXPERIENCE AND NO KNOWLEDGE.

I JUST SENT AN E-MAIL MESSAGE TO JAPAN. I DON'T KNOW THE LANGUAGE SO I TOOK YOUR ADVICE AND TYPED IT ALL IN CAPS.

WOW. THAT PUT IT ALL IN PERSPECTIVE.

CATBERT: EVIL H.R. DIRECTOR

ALICE YOU HAVE TO USE YOUR VACATION TIME OR YOU'LL LOSE IT.

BUT IF YOU TAKE TIME OFF, YOU'LL MISS YOUR DEADLINES. **HA HA HA HA HA HA!!!**

THIS IS EMBARRASSING. I LAUGHED MYSELF FUZZY.

IT'S A SHAME YOU HAVE TO WORK DURING YOUR VACATION. THE SAME THING HAPPENED TO ME.

REALLY?

ACTUALLY, IN MY CASE I WENT ON VACATION WHEN I WAS SUPPOSED TO BE WORKING. BUT THE CONCEPT IS THE SAME.

APPARENTLY SHE WASN'T LOOKING FOR EMPATHY.

I ADMIRE YOUR WORK ETHIC, ALICE. YOU'RE EVEN WORKING DURING YOUR VACATION.

IT MUST BE HARD TO REMAIN MOTIVATED WHEN YOU KNOW YOU CAN NEVER BREAK THROUGH THE GLASS CEILING.

SO, IT LOOKS LIKE IT'S JUST TILE AFTER ALL.

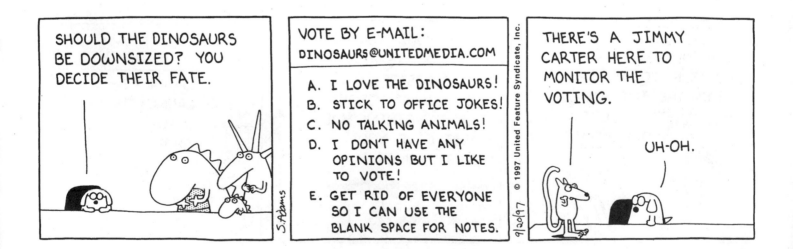

ALICE, I'VE NOTICED A DISTURBING PATTERN. YOUR SOLUTIONS TO PROBLEMS ARE ALWAYS THE THINGS YOU TRY LAST.

WITH ALL DUE RESPECT, ARE YOU USING YOUR SKULL TO STORE OLD RAGS OR WHAT?

IT'S A GOOD THING YOU SAID "WITH ALL DUE RESPECT."

I DISCOVERED THAT OUR POINTY-HAIRED BOSS DOESN'T KNOW HE'S BEING INSULTED IF YOU SAY "WITH ALL DUE RESPECT" FIRST.

I LOVE THE INTANGIBLE BENEFITS OF THIS JOB.

WITH ALL DUE RESPECT, IS THAT YOUR FACE OR IS A MONKEY CLIMBING DOWN YOUR COLLAR HEADFIRST?

CATBERT: EVIL H.R. DIRECTOR

I CAN'T RAISE YOUR SALARY LEVEL BECAUSE YOU DON'T HAVE TEN YEARS EXPERIENCE WITH "JAVA" CODING.

NOBODY HAS TEN YEARS EXPERIENCE WITH NEW TECHNOLOGY! YOU'RE JUST BEING EVIL. ADMIT IT.

AND COULD YOU PLEASE SHAKE YOUR HEAD BACK AND FORTH INSTEAD OF SPINNING IT AROUND?

Panel 1: CATBERT: EVIL H.R. DIRECTOR

THERE ARE SEVERAL MANDATORY CLASSES FOR MANAGERS.

Panel 2:
- AVOIDING CONTACT WITH SUBORDINATES.
- MISPLACING IMPORTANT DOCUMENTS.
- THE JOY OF LISTENING TO YOUR OWN VOICE.

Panel 3: HAVE YOU TAKEN THE PREREQUISITE CLASS IN TIME MANAGEMENT?

TWICE.

Panel 4: MANAGER TRAINING

NEVER BE IN THE SAME ROOM AS A DECISION.

DECISION

YOU

Panel 5: I'LL ILLUSTRATE MY POINT WITH A PUPPET SHOW THAT I CALL...

Panel 6: "JOURNEY TO BLAMEVILLE," STARRING "SUGGESTION SAM" AND "MANAGER MEG."

Panel 7: MANAGER TRAINING

YOU WILL OFTEN BE ASKED TO COMMENT ON THINGS YOU DON'T UNDERSTAND.

?

Panel 8: THESE HANDOUTS CONTAIN NONSENSE PHRASES THAT CAN BE USED IN ANY SITUATION.

Panel 9: ... SO, LET'S DOMINATE OUR INDUSTRY ... WITH QUALITY IMPLEMENTATION OF METHODOLOGIES.

I'LL GET RIGHT ON IT.